JESUS WALK WITH ME

BOOK 1

Donald G. Ennis

WRITERS REPUBLIC L.L.C.
515 Summit Ave. Unit R1
Union City, NJ 07087, USA

Website: *www.writersrepublic.com*
Hotline: *1-877-656-6838*
Email: *info@writersrepublic.com*

Ordering Information:
Quantity sales. Special discounts are available on quantity purchases by corporations, associations, and others. For details, contact the publisher at the address above.

Library of Congress Control Number: 2020909955
ISBN-13:   978-1-64620-392-5   [Paperback Edition]
                  978-1-64620-393-2   [Digital Edition]

Rev. date: 05/22/2020

This collection of my thoughts is about dreaming and not giving up.
It's about hope and prayer, when not feeling good about yourself.
Also, it is about finding strength and believing in God's timing.
I dedicate this book to the following:

Cadie Hockenbary

My pastor Donna Fitchette

My stepmom, Cathy

May this be the first of many books published every month.

Scary things happen to me and my life

Scary things are happening in the world and humanity for its sake is to change your life and your bad behavior because with God you know that God will come down to you today and always have your future look bright

Scary things don't say you are not going anywhere but up if you let the lesson learned from that moment you can see the beauty of this action

Scary thing is that we are in need of you making them just a little more less scary than we thought we might find

Scary things happen to you today and always have perspective on this issue because you are the basis and Christ will give you your victory…too and your life will help us all stay together for the sake of our humanity

DON'T LET THE WIND IN MY HEART OR MIND
    DISTRACT ME
FROM WHAT STARTED
DON'T HAVE THE RIGHT DIRECTION OF HIS PLAN
HIS ANGELS WILL BRING YOU HOME
LET ME SEE THE DIFFERENCE BETWEEN THE TWO
    AND THREE
DIFFERENT THINGS
THAT MEANS THAT YOU HAVE THE SAME PROBLEM
    EVERY DAY
YOU WILL KNOW WHAT TO HANG ON TO AND LET
    GO BY GOD'S GRACE...
ALL THINGS ARE MEANT TO LOOK AT AND
    MOVE ON...

DON'T LET THE ENENY WIN
DON'T LET THEM KNOW WHAT YOU THINK
DON'T LET THEM CRUSH YOUR SPIRIT
DON'T LET THEM WIN
DON'T LET THE ENEMY take your passion

DON'T QUESTION YOUR DECISION
DON'T QUESTION YOUR HEART
DON'T QUESTION YOUR FUTURE
DON'T QUESTION YOUR FAITH
DON'T QUESTION YOUR LIFE

Don't question his work
Don't question his why
Don't question his ways
Give God your faith
Give God your belief
Give God the foundation
Give God the world to heal
Give me your wisdom and your life so you can see the light in my eyes
Give me the faith in mankind that we are going forward with your heart

BELIEVE

I believe in Jesus
I do
Believe in the promise
I do
Believe in the truth
I do
Believe in the cure
I do
Believe in the moment
I do
Believe the way you deliver your life
And that he won't waver from you
I do
Believe in you
I do
Believe in your dreams
I do

I believe in this world
I do
I believe in the universe
I do
I believe Jesus loves me
I do
Even when I am screwing up
I do
Even when I am mad at him
I do
But he says I love you my son
I do
You are forgiven
You are
You are my light
You are
I create you
You did
Inperfected
I am
No doubt
I have my savior
And you stop doubting
Will my father

DONALD G. ENNIS

IT'S NOT ALWAYS EASY
I FIND MYSELF CAUGHT
BETWEEN
THE GOD WAY AND MAN'S WAY
TUGGING
YET KNOW WHO WINS EVERYTIME
IT'S NOT THE STRUGGLE
OF KNOWING
IT'S THERE
BUT IT'S THE DURATION
THAT GETS THE BEST OF ME MOST OF THE TIME

God has a big plan for my life. He always has, and yet in my flesh it gets lost. I spend too much time worrying and comparing myself. I let man and the here and now be the focal point. Now mind you, God is always with me, but he gets drowned out. He loves me anyway. So this must put Him in prime view. Never let a second go without thinking, thanking, praying. So today I decided to follow and pursue dreams, take action, and live one day at a time. For God knows my days and the number. He will fulfill them and all that are part of my destiny.

PRAYER

Father, you remind me that it is never too late
Never too late to recharge your heart
Never too late to recharge your passion
Never too late to rethink the situation
Never too late to start talking about the house of God
Never let the enemy win over the house of God
Never mind the one who gives you heartache
But rely on the house of God
God live in me and you reveal your heart
May my heart beat
May my mind find a calm river flow
Where images of you are my picture
And it's beautiful

PRAYERS

For the world
Amen
For the human spirit
Amen
For our neighbor
Amen
For our brother and sisters
Amen
For the enemy we are facing now to subside
Amen
For the health of all to receive the benefit of the house of God
Amen

PRAYER

To my Heavenly Father
Many are scared
Rest their mind
Rest their fears
Rest the uncertainty

Hope for new release from the end of my grip
Hope for the release of the enemy stronghold
Let his grip weaken
Let the world be better THAN tomorrow
We are in crisis
We are in desperate need of miracles
Turn to you
In every moment
In every tear
That falls
Every worry that we have
God bless us
We never known what in store
We were living foolishly
Just getting by
In means of blinders
We were moving
Not realizing
The enemy was in the air
He was ready
He knew we break
We would fall to pieces

The news is depressive
Little light
It's there really is
In snip bits
But it's there
My mission is to change the direction of the human spirit
Help me to keep my eyes open and honest with the world
Let them know what you want me to do
Alpha is the only one who gives you the sky and you can see the difference in your life
Jesus, make me yours for the world and humanity.
Just got a little longer to go to God for the house of God with all His love for you

MAY FIND THE SIMPLE BRIGHT SPOT FOR THE HOUSE OF GOD AND THE TRUTH DOES SET UP FOR THE PEOPLE TO REALIZE THEY ARE IN HIS NAME
HIS NAME HAS BEEN MISSING SINCE THE BEGINNING BUT HE DOES NOT LET YOU DOWN AND KEEP YOUR EYES OPEN FOR THE REST OF THE HOUSE OF GOD TO HEAL THE WORLD

Where are you going forward with the house of God
And He will restore all that you need Him to fulfill for you always
Know what you want me to do with my life and your life will help us understand what we are Going forward with the truth does

REALIZATION

In my human flesh I am so easily ready to place blame. To point a finger. Now mind you, I was one who put myself in the problem. I spent too much or went overboard, letting the enjoyment of stuff become more important than common sense. Instead of enjoying and using what I already have, I would just get more. Now I have more books than I've read, more CDs than I can listen to, more scarves than I can wear, and more DVDs than I can watch. Now I am not saying you can't have these things or can't enjoy them, yet it's the enjoyment and the use that's more important than the number. They are meant for pleasure and not the assumption. There are many who would love a third of what I have in these man-made pleasures. I am thankful for them.

Prayer: Lord, may you remind me that enjoyment over assumption is the way to go.

Thought: Read one book before moving on to another. Watch DVDs weekly. Wear scarves often. Listen to music daily.

Reminder: Enjoy what you have, and before you add more, ask yourself this: do I need it now?

DREAMS

We live and we forget how to dream. We get caught up in the every day. We feel we are too old or we left people dictate our future.

God gave us a life to live. Not run a rat race. He does not create human life to run and not know peace of mind in our day. When we don't dream, then we go through a routine. Now, yes, in the here and now we have to, because that is the way we live. We take on and do so much, but do so little. We are living for the flesh and not the soul. By doing this, we put a limit on our mind and a restless feeling on our body. So this I say to you: dream and let God hear you.

Prayer: God, pray that I never lose my ability to dream. Always put my dreams in your hands.

Thought: Dreams are meant to keep the mind active and fresh. Always dream big and small. Always know they can be big and small, simple and complex. Dreaming to me is always hopeful. It's a reminder that you are alive. You were born to dream. You can dream, but there is a reality you must know. You must know there is a practical view.

Realization: You can't fulfill a dream if you aren't active. You can't just dream and then wishfully think it will happen.

Practical Approach: Give it to God. Be active daily. Have a game plan. Never give up. Have faith. Work hard. Be diligent.

THE WHY

Why: Why do I let people control my fate?

Thought: Because I have been conditioned from an early age as well as a result of my upbringing.

Prayer: Lord, you are in control of my days and my life. Only you can bring what is meant to be. Only you can be the Master. You have a final say on the how and the number of my days.

Realization: I am not being true to God. I must and want to be more authentic in all of my days to you.

Why: Why is it hard for me to believe in myself? Why is it so hard to follow through?

Thought: I was raised to not believe and not to dream, to only accept man's plans for and on my life.

Prayer: Lord, Your will be done. You decide what is real and what matters. You have the answer.

Realization: When we put it in God's hands, He will be enough. When you stop needing social media approval and man's, then, and only then, can you be free.

Why: Why do I go back and forth in my daily ambition? Why does my focus stray?

Thought: Maybe because in a world of "now" and not "later," we get bored and get distracted easily.

Prayer: Father, help me to stay on the prize and your Kingdom. Let me know you are never away from me.

Realization: Pray.

One day at a time.

Never look back.

Trust in Jesus.

Breathe.

Focus.

Why: Why does it seem like I'm worried today? I was so worried about how to get through the week and why he has to struggle. Is it my fault?

Prayer: Thank you for doing what you do best. Thank you for love and grace. You came through and were always in awe. How do you come through even in prayers we don't say aloud? You amaze me.

Thought: True story about a recent situation. He was broke. Only $25 dollars to his name. Buys a five-dollar ticket and wins $500.00.

Realization: Make a decision.

Set a goal.

Put into action.

Focus.

Want to change.

Don't repeat.

Why: Why do I want to cry the night before? Why do I get physically ill thinking about the next day?

Thought: Because it is not doing Your work. It's not being real to myself. Goes against everything I am not.

Prayer: Place me where I am meant to be. Your will be done. Make me the man I'm meant to be.

Realization: Be thankful.

All this is temporary.

Do your best.

Remember what He has given you.

Breathe.

Bring it to God.

True Event: Was at the grocery store. Left my wallet on the counter and my keys as well. Money and cards were in my wallet.

God's Intervention: No money was missing. All cash intact. No cards missing. Keys next to the wallet.

Realization: God exists, looks out for me.

Why: Why does it not always work out as planned?

Thought: We do it to ourselves. We don't think. We give into flesh. We try to do it our way.

Prayer: Help me to lean on you. Help me to relax. Help me to see the bigger picture. Help me to focus on your ways.

Realization: I don't have all the answers. I must not play God. If it's not God's way, then it's not worthy of doing. I know that I must study.

Why: Why does it hurt when we lose someone?

Thought: Natural feeling. We want to control the outcome. We want to be the gatekeeper. We try to tell God how long and when someone enters or leaves us.

Prayer: Father, help me to know that loss is a part of life and the journey. Remind me that you are the one who controls the number of days.

Realization: God heals.

God knows and will reserve the timing.

God knows you.

This too shall pass.

Why: Why do I forget who I was meant to be?

Thought: I listen to the wrong voice in my head. I don't have faith in myself. I live in a world where comparison runs rampant. I look to the wrong source to feel worthy.

Prayer: May you be the source that fuels my destiny. May I have the faith needed to do my best. May I not need to compare and always feel worthy in your word.

Realization: He will make me in his vision. When I put God first, he will set the final destination into my path. When I give my cares to my master, then I will be in the right place. Look to God for who I am. Look to His ways and be set free. Love the flaws because they are God-given. Man only judges you, and yet God creates a masterpiece.

Why: How do we find a better way to come together?

Thought: We read the Bible from front to back. We study it book by book. We never put biased thoughts and replace God's words. We listen to the stories of those who have been changed by the grace of God. We remember we have the same color blood. When we bleed, it is the same color—red. We unite on a daily basis. Pray that we see our enemy as our brother and sister in Christ. Realize that it is easier said than done. We can only change our hearts first. Then we can help others. Pray that hate is erased for the next generation. We must come together as one, one step at a time. Realize that when judgment day comes, only God will be the judge and jury. Pray for a day that we can love without any biases. Realize your potential in God.

Always know the root of what is bothering you. Be real and admit the source of your negative thoughts. When you do this, it makes the whys in life less likely to come up.

Now not saying they won't come up. You just won't see them as much. When they do, they won't weigh so heavily on your mind. Nor will they rob you of your day and waste time always thinking of "Why me?" Why can't this or that be? You can focus more on others and how to change the world.

Prayer: Instead of thinking, *Why me?* teach me to think how I cannot repeat.

SCRIPTURE REFLECTIONS

I call on you, O God, for you will answer me.
Give ear to me and hear my prayer. (Ps.17: 6)

God always hears us. No matter if you are quiet or yell or cry or just utter, "God, help me." He knows your pain, and he knows my joy. Yet we sometimes will ask and receive something we later regret. God always answers me. Learned the hard way to make sure that when I ask, it comes from an honest and real place. God will even sometimes give you something to prove His point. He wants you to know that He knows the why and if you are ready for the destiny He lined up for you so long ago..

When you make a vow to God, do not delay
in fulfilling it. He has no pleasures in fools.
(Eccles. 5:4)

When you give a dream to God, He is not interested in fancy words or the act of using your tongue. He wants to see you mean it. He won't do His part and just wave a wand while saying, "It will be done." He wants to see your commitment. He wants to see your actions. He always wanted you to mean it. With God, it's a two-way street. If you put in the time and honest effort, then your Savior will bring to light what is meant to be.

Zophar: My troubled thoughts prompt me to
answer because I am greatly disturbed. (Job
20:2)

When you hang on to thoughts too long, they will consume you. They will have an effect on every area of your life. You spend too much time on you and not others. You were meant to laugh, love, and live. Not meant to always be about you. Let God handle it. After all, He is the Alpha. Always breathe in and say, "God, help me." It's simple, and He is ready to listen and help you go forward. Leggo. Handle your battle and you live. Best way is to take one day at a time. For me, I repeat, "God, help me," daily.

> When I think about this, I am terrified,
> trembling seizes my body. (Job 21:6)

Many times I overthink and plan. I make steps and then rethink them. I alter my actions and make adjustments. It's daily and time-consuming. Yes, no rest for the wicked, but even more wasted energy for the thinker. Recently, I've been trying to take one day at a time. Keep it simple. Still a daily process but it's a little more peaceful. Can find some joy in everyday life. When I get too close to that line of action and obsession, then I pray this: "God, help me. You're the Alpha and I am merely human." God bless you.

> Let not those gloat over me, who are my enemies
> without cause. (Ps.35:19)

No one should ever judge me, nor assume anything about me. We all get judged. That is truly only God's duty. Even if I have been so-called giving them reason to, again, only God judges me. People should always want to know why. What is the reason or the background story that makes us do what we do? Where does it say I live for man? Yet man always wants to have the answer or at best play God. They feel they have the right to judge me. In the end God says, "I am the way."

I cried out to God for help! I cried out to God
to hear me. (Ps. 77:1)

The cried-out part in this has never been more true. I have what is
called monthly meltdowns. I cry to the point where I get sick. I hold
too much worry in and try to fix myself. Yet know that God wants to
take my pain. He hears me even when I yell and say dumb things. He
never forsakes me. I love how that feels. Not the meltdown, mind you.
But the fact God will always remain in me. God will always be mine
and will be free of Satan.

My responsibility to my creator:
Ask and receive.
Knock and seek.
Have faith.
Trust in His word.
Study His word.
Share His world.

God's promise to me:
Never forsake me.
Always make each day new day to improve.
Will love me unconditionally.
Will always guide me to the destiny that awaits me.

My promise to the readers:
Be candid and real.
Share my experiences.
Write from the heart.
Always to encourage.

I forgot how to dream and hope like a child. The more I get into your world and your word, I can be a dreamer. I can hope again and know that even if they are different dreams, they are still a dream. They are hope for what comes next in life. They also can be the simple and the biggest. They will be a reality and a place to be with you. So I will share my recent dreams. Will allow my mind to be open and adjust to where my journey has led me to know. The dreams are your will. You make their reality the best way and the way that is right for me. For if tell you, then they are demands and not dreams.

I wake up every morning. Instead of it being about God, it's about regret. Why should it be regret when God gave me what I wanted? I got the position I wanted. Could be I am human and never satisfied. Yes, but also I am not fulfilling my dream. My desire to do more and be more. Have I settled for less? When you are doing what you have to and living for flesh, then you gave up dreaming. You are just going through the motions, yet you are not really living. This makes God very sad. You were put here to dream and live a life full of joy. So I urge you to dream again and let your light shine again. Whatever makes you unhappy will pass. Glory to God.

> For now I would be lying down in peace.I would
> be asleep and at rest. (Job3:13)

I rarely dream at night. Yet this verse brings me to a peaceful place. You can dream anywhere and anytime, just like you talk to God. We need rest to be our best. We need dreams to feel alive.

Prayer: Father, may You meet me at the place, the place where I can dream and feel at ease. May our minds be one and not restless. This is my prayer to you.

> Why is light given to those in misery, and life
> to the bitter of soul. (Job 3:20)

Love this verse. It has depth and really hits home. We need the light to heal and grow. Just as living things need light to grow, so do we need the light to push ahead. To dream, we need the hope of a better day. We need to see a better outlook. To me, the light represents finding God when you are at the lowest depths of misery.

Life to the bitter soul. For me, feeling this is what keeps me going. As much as I feel down and ready to give up, remember I am alive and feeling something. Reminded that no matter my discomfort with my emotions, when God puts light on my bitter soul, then there is always hope. As long as I feel, then know I am alive to dream and see a better day. Rather feel something than nothing at all.

I apply this verse in the following way:

Light never fails to bring an end to the darkness.

Light shines ever in the places you think are dead.

Life gives the soul an alternative feeling to focus on rather than staying bitter.

Life will always have its bad days. Yet you never have to stop dreaming or stay bitter.

All hard work brings a profit, but mere talk leads only to poverty. (Prov.1:23)

I tend to speak a lot. I say out loud my dreams and confess to God. I also know He listens, but He loves when I am actually consistent, when I actually do something, that brings me closer to the outcome I want or dream about. When I say it and am active, He will make a way. My dream comes true.

He gives me the plan. I know how to achieve, and I am good at staying on target. Okay, most of the time. I know the procedure and how to. Now just gotta keep on the prize. The part about poverty also brings real ties into my life. When you make a plan, you know God will approve and you say it. You even speak out loud yet you backtrack. You're good for a few days, then you slack off. You hear God saying, "What happened?" Then you speak and say out loud, "I gotta get back on track." You also know that you put blinders on and go, "If I say it, then it must work." Well, not really, because I am here to say, you'd be surprised. You end up at the same place while only moving in a false state. You are broke, money and spirit wise. So in a matter of saying, do what I try: say what you mean and mean what you say.

MY DREAM PLAN

Mean what I say.

Say what I mean.

Stay focused.

When I say it not only say it, but put it into action.

Once you begin doing the steps that bring you closer to the dream, make sure you keep going.

Always implement on a daily basis.

Be vigilant on what you do.

Prayer: Lord, as I write this devotional, may words pour out from my soul.

Thought: Same book title, three-part trilogy, devotional journal prayer book

FURTHER SCRIPTURAL PONDERINGS

The tongue that brings healing is a tree of life,
but a deceitful tongue crushes the spirit. (Prov.
15:4)

The first part of the verse makes me think that when you give a kind word to someone who hurts, that you heal the soul, that you encourage the soul. You also bring new hope to them. When someone gives up or stops dreaming and you say or speak an encouraging word, you help them to believe and dream again. You are a healer with your words. You can bring life into a dark place and make a dream revise itself. The second part of the verse is very deep to me as well. To me, it says don't say things that are not true. Don't repeat what people think or what you Satan wants you to believe. I also feel that when I read this verse, the second part speaks to me. When you focus on the negative and repeat it, you will crush your spirit. You will not only give power to Satan, but you will always be stuck. You will never know peace because you are what you think. Remember what and who God made you to be. Only say the right thoughts that God speaks to you.

Prayer: God let me always speak life and never crush my spirit

Commit to the Lord whatever you do and your
plans will succeed. (Prov.16:3)

Love this verse. For many reasons, it speaks to me. I love what it promises. I love what it says in just a few short words. It gives me the openness to dream, more than just wishful thinking. I can make a plan, be active, and take steps, then watch it come to be by His will and grace. He makes the reality of words into actual reality. Oh, how I love Jesus and future dreams.

> Do not boast about tomorrow for you do not
> know what a day brings forth. (Prov.27:1)

When I read this, I feel as if they are saying to me live in the moment and not ignore today. You can dream but don't lose sight of the day in front of you. You don't wanna get so caught up in a dream that you lose sight of the blessings you have right in front of you. Feel as though that's where a lot of my stress comes from. Know God will get me there. Only He knows the number of my days.

Random thought on this verse: Feel as though I need to concentrate as I write my devotional.

DREAM-RELATED THOUGHTS

Dreams are gifts from God and are meant to keep you focused on hope.

Dreams are a waste if you are not going to have a plan.

Dreams require you to put in motion steps and be active.

Apply a day-to-day mind-set.

Dreams give you hope and they provide a new outlook for your life.

Dreams should never be squashed for it's God's pleasure for you to dream.

Dreams are the best way to stay close to God. They keep you in a consistent talk with God.

Dreams are the key to a healthy spirit. They keep the Devil at bay and they are way to stay positive.

Dreams require an action plan. They are a day-to-day activity. They are meant to be any size in the concept. Speak them often.

Dreams can cover any area. They are not just a one-trick pony. You can dream anywhere and about anything.

Dreams hold on to them. No one can ever say or tell you not to dream. You are born with a childlike mind. Don't dream like an adult with limits. Use your new dreams to feel alive and be an inspiration.

Dream no one dream is the same as anyone else's. Dare to dream your dream and not compare it.

There is a time for everything and a season for
activity under the heavens. (Eccles.3:3)

When I read this, I have always felt before I knew this verse. Very
true and a well-respected verse. Had to end this section with it.

My personal prayer and request for dreams:

Prayer to be debt free.

Prayer to pay off the car.

Pray to work, write, and travel promoting my devotionals. I
want to be a writer. God's will.

GOD, HUMANS ARE MENTAL YET YOU ARE PEACE!

Lord, lay me down to sleep, bring me a restful night. May my night be full of You. I cast my worries to You.

Sleep - Don't rob me of my sleep. May instead it be a time to rest and wake up ready for the new day my Savior has prepared.

Sleep - When I close my eyes, it's to be with Jesus. It's my time to forget my day. A time to repent and ask for forgiveness.

Sleep - You are my intimate time with my creator. Amen.

POETIC PRAYERS

Nighttime
Lay me down
Close my eyes
Turn off the sound
Only hear you
Give it away
And seal it in you
Meet me there
Find the place
Where it's solid
Where no noise distracts
And we are one
Give me rest
Give me sleep
Deep and soothing
We meet now
Ready to dream
And find my sleep
As lay me down
Close my eyes
No more thoughts
Drift away
And call it quits
I am one with sleep
This I pray in your name

Morning

Wake from a restless sleep
A sleep that seems not solid
I hear the sounds of the day beginning
The thoughts start to wander in my head
When I speak first words out loud
They are to thee, to you my father
God be with me
Silence the noise
Get me through this day
Help me to remember
It's dark when I awake
Not only in the mental, but in the spirit
Help me to see the light
Where all is good
Where the road seems real
And we walk together
Hand in hand
God be with me
Now and forever. Amen.

SCARED

Lord, I often get scared about how I will survive by myself. Not because I don't have you yet. It's the fact that let men be who I depended on. I put my trust in men and not my Savior who is the only true man that will provide. Love that about my Creator. That no matter what, I can reach out to You and You answer.

Prayer: God, be with me at all times. Hear my cries to You. Reach out and hold my heart. Put me in the place I belong as You mold me. Let me know and always feel that love and bond. Amen.

REGRET

Never hang on to what has been. You were meant to learn and move on. You are allowed to feel it but again never meant to own it. When you hang on or own it, then it festers and holds you down. You are not a slave to its hold. Let God break the chain we call regret. As human beings, we can give it to God and walk away. He will replace the regret with a peace and joy like you've never known.

Prayer: Lord, never let regret consume me or my heart. Break all chains and fill my inner peace. Let the new life settle in my heart. Amen.

> Give ear to my words, Oh Lord consider my sighing. (Ps.5:1)
>
> Listen to my cry for help my king and my God for to you I pray. (Ps.5:2)
>
> In the morning, Oh Lord, You hear my voice. In the morning I lay my request before you and wait in expectation. (Ps.5:3)
>
> How long, oh Lord will you forget me forever? How long will you hide your face from me? (Ps.13:1)
>
> How long must I wrestle with my thoughts? And every day have sorrow in my heart. How long will my enemy triumph over me? (Ps.13:2)
>
> I will sing to the Lord for he has been good to me. (Ps.13:6)

RANDOM POINTS

Never have regrets in your life.

Never be scared about anything. Instead, give it to God.

At night dream with and about God's plans for your life.

In the morning say, "God, what will this day bring?" Put your first words into a positive realm. When you do any other way, you set the failure into motion. You are almost sure to let him slide in the negative. Satan will love this and will use it to his advantage. Don't give him any more energy than he has already stolen.

> I will praise the Lord, who counsels me even at
> night my heart instructs me. (Ps.16:7)

Really love how it promises a boundary that can't be forsaken. Where you and God are one in the body, mind, and soul. Where the love and safety are yours from God and never leaves. You can count and always call out to Him.

Areas where I feel this verse most:

My destiny - God's will

My outlook when scared - God's safety

My sleepless night - God's calmness

My everyday struggle - God's security

My family - when missing them

My future - when dreaming again

ENTREATIES TO GOD

Lord, I look
I see helpless man
Can't take it away
The pain is not mine to take
Only you can do so
I am asking this of you.

I am struggling here
My emotions say and feel hurt
My mind says the money
Where and how will pay
Sickness of the fact that
Though comes up at all
Reality is not have I yet to make the market my income
    let alone my extra source of income.

My heart say need to take care of him
Will have to step up to ensure he will eat better
To ensure he drinks more liquid.
Will also need to keep me up.
Keep my spirit and rive up
Will require more sleep, exercise, and diet change
Focus on investments
Generate more income all for the sake of him
Need to rise up and be the man
You made me strong and here is my chance to prove to world
Show you I am ready for the life I have been asking for.

Let me the man you have designed

Rise up and say no to the devil.

Say no to fear just waiting to knock me down.

Say yes to heal him

In my power at hand, praise you for doing the miracle.

Need that miracle

For there is a time coming

Reality never really gives you a break

But it does not have to break you

You will always face the moment when you decide to fall or stand

A time to be weak or victorious

When you know emotions be heavy

Cloud your mind-set

Yet you have to push through

Let it be known in Jesus' name

Where you are going

Why you want it

And you trust God to give it to you

A miracle is not just wishful thinking, but faith.

When it's all said and done

We begin again

Important to praise and declare in God's name

To say out loud your declaration.

For me it's hard, but not for obvious reasons

Yet because have many and know God wants to hear all of them

He wants to make all come true

Yet wants me to trust and have faith that He will deliver so I praise Him

I give my worries to him.

I trust He will use my test and pass me with flying colors

For cannot fail my God

It's not written in our deal.

Lord, hear me now
I come to thee asking why?
Yet already deep down know my what
The reason my thoughts are my enemy
Why my circumstance brings my soul
As I look, knock, and seek
You will show, open, and will receive what is meant to be
With my action it will happen
In your time it will come to rest
In my actions it will progress
May you never leave it undone
Let the triumphs blow loud
As I make my promise
To thee, oh Heavenly Father
What to do to him am I
If I am not taking care of
Mentally need to focus on you
Physically need to be example of all health
More exercise, sleep, food, and positive energy
Emotionally be vigilant in my pursuit
Stay determined
Spiritually the less on my mind, the more can focus on him
Reduce my stress
Pay off my car
Stock market my income
Generate growing income
Allows me to focus on him
Give him more attention
You will take care of my needs
This I know to be true
Because I pray to you.

HOME NOW

Where can recharge
So ask You to not let Satan visit me while I am open to his attempts
Instead recharge my mind and keep eye on the final destination
See this is where I write
Where study your word and bring my books to life
This is where my income from market will be generated
This where I will pay my debt off
This where I will pay my car off
Where will be the man meant to be
Where the quiet time is mine to touch base with you
Will continue to pray my request
Debt free
Own my car
Day trader income
Earn a nonstop income while the rest will be his care
And putting him before me
Will have a balance
Will have all areas in their place
Each time precious and more connection

One won't be more than other or more less they all come together as one
As plan well crafted and driven by You
The one who makes all come true
Will you not hear my words as pour out my confessions
We forget we are loved
We get focused on our daily lives
We move with the fast pace
Yet God will remind us of love and how much
Sadly it's usual in a test, but that's okay
We forget our strength
We get focused on things doing well
We don't tap into it on a sunny day
And when we need it the devil says oh no wait
It will cloud our emotions and our vision
To see spiritually and even literally
He wants to break us
He wants to say my way better
Yet only God is the way.

NO MORE

With my recent scare
I say no more
I am ready to take on
the evil ways of man
and the one who tries to steal my thunder

Say no more fear
I will trust in God
No more worry the funny and the lesson
No more will he rob me
Only what God will bring me into
My road to the destiny am supposed to be on
Not the train of self-doubt

No more fear
No more whys
NO more I can't
No more I am not
No more it's not easy
No more it's too hard

More yes to I am strong
More yes to don't always have to have an answer
More yes I can do all things through Christ Jesus
More yes to I am capable
More yes to the test and the lesson
More yes to the struggle, for without it I can't remind myself
    what I am made of

I love you, O Lord, my Strength. (Ps.18:1)

Will pray this every day with the Father's Prayer.
Praise God my Savior and salvation.

Today I am thankful for the following:
My job
My family
My friends
The love that surrounds me
The mind to stay focused
My cats
The love of Jesus
The day lesson
The breath take all day
The tears to release pain
The destiny that awaits
The beauty in life
The writing of my books
Publication
The sleep I'm about to receive
The promise from God
God's story
My health
My diligence
The way that He made me
The love of friends

A man can do nothing better than to eat and
drink and find in his work. This too, I see, is
from the hand of God. (Eccles.2:24)

We live in a world of rush, where we have to be better. We don't enjoy and just live in the moment. We have a fast-paced daily routine. We never slow down and enjoy the simple little things. The wind in your hair. The purr of the family cat. The sun rays as they shine. In this verse God says, "Eat." So eat and be healthy. Now he doesn't say eat and no exercise, then complain you are overweight. He says, "Eat." You were meant to eat food; for it nourishes the body, mind, and soul. You eat and then move and God takes care of your body image. You don't need to worry about the body image or let man be the judge. God knows what you are to look like. He says what the temple is supposed to look like on the inside and outside. He knows what shape and what curves the temple has.

I don't drink, but I do want to find satisfaction in my work. So for me, I want to do my very best. Be happy and know I give my all when I perform my job duties. Usually, I have to pray in these areas:

Pray to do my best

Pray I can perform

Pray that though everything is temporary; it's still important

Pray to get through and not grumble

Pray that it's not a chore

Pray to do what I must

Pray to know it's part of the journey

Pray that I get my mind active

Pray that it is not easy, yet not hard to fulfill

Pray to my Heavenly Father

When you do something, enjoy, find the satisfaction in all you do. Let it be known to God you are doing for Him and then you do for others. Others can do for you as well, yet it should be for satisfaction and not from selfish nor from an ego mind-set.

Pray to find the joy
Pray to find enjoyment
Pray find recharge
Pray to find my calling
Pray to find peace
Pray to find a humble aura

Thankful for earthly things. Earthly things don't define me. They are meant to bring joy. They are meant to bring a humble feeling. To you, my Lord, I pray.

Looks, God-given gift. We all look the way Jesus says. Some has a unique look. Others are a pretty package. Instead of using them to deceive, to manipulate people into doing things or lying and pretending, you have depth. We need to cherish it because you age. True beauty and sexiness is in your behavior and how you treat people. They are never forever. They will fade and all you have is character. So if you're pretty, people, remember that the time capsule is cruel. So be kind and enjoy the looks why they last. God hates vanity.

I am not gorgeous, but God gave me a tender heart for the world and to be an example of love. To be human first and a source of love. I am not sexy. I am just me. For me, sexy is a feeling, which is a result of how you carry with your fellow man. For me, gorgeous is having a heart and soul that always puts human race before his own needs. For me, loving what I see in the mirror is far better than fancy words and empty compliments.

It's in the how, not when you get there. For me, it's about Jesus and his way. The simplicity of prayer and action. One step at a time, always asking God, praying his Father's prayer. Seeking his wisdom, knowing no matter what, he has always provided. He has always come through for me. I have always believed that long before I was intimate with Jesus.

His voice soothes me

His love saves me

His Word is the walkway

He comforts me

He knows my every need

He walks beside me

He gives me strength

I turn to my alpha, Jesus

Psalm10:1 and 2:

> The Lord says to my lord sit at my right hand
> until I make your enemies a foot stool for your
> feet.

(Point: Never fear your doubters nor your naysayers. Hold fast in Jesus)

> The Lord will extend your mighty scepter from
> Zion you will rule in the midst of your enemies.

(Point: Trust God. Ask and receive. Seek and find. Bring God your cares. Believe in the Father. Don't worry. Be active with God. Love no matter what.)

I will declare that your love stands firm forever
that you establish your faithfulness in heaven
itself. (Ps. 89:2)

Reflection: I will always need Jesus as will you. I will always try to hold his will above my own. Will always turn to God over mere men and the world's ways. You can have eternal life. The flesh merely a temple for which the spirit is covered by for the here and now.

Pray to Jesus every day and leave no part of your life untouched.

Hear, oh Lord, and answer me for I am poor
and needy. (Ps.86:1)

Reflection: The Lord will provide. He has prosperity lined up. He will replace needy with sense of fulfillment. He will always delight to hear from me and you. When you ask, you will receive. When you seek, you will find.

Prayer: Lord, never forsake me. Never leave me behind in the world's battle of struggle. Give me your ear and grace.

Reflection Recap:
  Dream again.
  Pray always.
  Give God your worries.
  Let love in.
  Be open to His call.
  Share His word.

Inspire others.
Let love win.
Ask God.
Pray to God.
Don't give up.
Believe in your words.
Speak it to God.
Mean what you say and He will make it happen.
Look to no other, but God himself.
Be ready to walk with the Majestic One.
Give unto Jesus always.
Bring no doubt into life.
Give your best.
Be honest with where you are.

Love devotionals

Love writing

It's a way to clear your mind

You can replace the evil one's destruction

You can have a better mind-set

When you write or read someone else's words, you can relate

Deep down we all wanna be heard

Good, bad, and the ugly

You can get a new perspective on an issue you are dealing with

Closing prayer:

    May my words help.

    May my books relax you.

    May God let me write devotionals.

    May God come alive through my devotionals.

Proverbs 1:2–19

Reflection:

Do not follow others. Do not do what the crowd does, because in the end it's not the Jesus' way. People will deceive you for their own gain and desires. When you let stuff consume and not enjoy, they rob you. You can't take it with you. When you want something and ask for it, then make you are coming from an honest and godly place. Be careful what you wish for, and be humble in asking.

Proverbs 1:20–24

Reflection:

We are meant to dream and turn to God. We were meant to rise above the ordinary and live out a destiny from Him. God gives us the way and the truth. If you listen and look, He not only restores them literally but spiritually to live better. God doesn't wait for your to decide nor does he do it all for you. He expects you to be active and do your part. With God, you ask and receive and seek and find. He wants you to trust Him in life.

WORDS

They have power.

Strong as weapons and steel.

They have ability to heal, hurt, and inspire.

Words are new weapon.

They are used casually and not much thought goes into them
most of the time.

Yes, we have freedom of speech.

Yet God warns about the power of the tongue.

May you use your words.

May you use them wisely.

Words, communication are always the best way.

So now let's pray:

Words, may you use them. Words are the voice of God.

LOVE

Love is the key.
It moves mountains.
We read about it.
We sing about it.
It's the gift that never stops giving.
Love today.
Love tomorrow.
Love every day.
Don't go a day without love.
God's biggest command says love.
Love thy neighbor as I love you.
He wants you to love.
He wants us all to love.
We need to love.
We are meant to give it away.
Fill your heart.
No matter what God loves.
When you love, be His love machine.
Love.
Love and more love.

LIFE

Live it well.

Never squander it away.

Each new day God chooses to bring you closer to His destiny for you.

Life.

It's meant to experience the pleasure.

Learn from the pain.

Grow with your faith.

Life.

Never easy or promised there would be no trials, but God gave you life.

He gave up His for you.

Life.

Looks at you.

Says ready or not, I am happening.

So what do you do?

Pray to God.

Be active.

Grow and learn.

Then God says it's your life.

BREATHE

When you breathe, you release the pressure of the day.

You invite new life into your soul.

You are to breathe and not hold it in.

Let your stress go.

Breathe.

Where you feel the pressure, take a deep breath in and out,
    then say "God, you are in me."

You are my air supply.

You will give me new life.

Breathe.

It's easy.

It's a stress release.

You do it daily.

Why not be thankful for each new day?

As you breathe, praise God for your life.

FATE

Do we end up where we are supposed to be?
Or do we end up where choices lead us?
We all make choices in life.
The key is not to let them turn into regret.
Maybe the best way is to not repeat the same choices.
Do your best.
I am not totally perfect at doing it myself.
I try to make the best of it.
Life and people get in the way.
Fate.
Not sure about it.
Even I question God on why he does it.
If I shall have a destiny, is it grand in my dreams?
Or is it the reality of my day?

WHY

Instead of asking why, say to God, "I will listen. I will do my part."

Won't question.

Will instead believe there is a reason.

God already knows so don't worry and get worked up.

But instead just do what you can.

Give it an honest attempt.

Pray daily.

Look to Him for an answer.

Take one day at a time.

One step at a time.

Don't run.

Don't try to fast track.

We have too many whys in our life.

Let's drop some now.

Relax.

Give it to God.

No more whys, just yes to God.

KNOW

You can know what you want.
You can know what you must do.
Yet you must know to give it to God.
You must know that you have to be active.
God knows what your desires are in your heart.
Know.
I now know what my calling is.
Know enough, I can't just give lip service.
I must do what I have to.
Know what my options are.
Will be active and do what I need to.
Knowing is only half the battle.
Prayers, faith, and God those are the rest.
This must and now know.

I was weak.

I was lost.

Never far from you.

I was scared.

I cried out to you.

You heard me.

Never forsaking me.

You're my Lord.

I love thee more than myself.

Always wanted.

Trying to be best me.

I was.

I'm not really sure, but his I know, you give me more and for that you are Lord.

Father.

Forgive me again.

I am only human.

I was weak.

No more.

I was lost, but found thee.

Never far from you.

Amen.

G O D

Was a bit shaky.
You gave me a gift.
You gave me Cadie when I needed an ear and a soundboard.
When I needed a friend.
You gave me real human connections.
You love me.
I see that now.
Thank you for my Cadie.
Thank you for my friend.
A voice to communicate.
A set of eyes to see fully and set of ears to hear your truth.
Thank you for my life; crazy, but full of promise life.
May you always be my rock of salvation in my heart.

Lord, the world wants to shake me.
Yet you say no.
I choose to say not now devil.
God has my heart.
His love will give me vision to see, ears to listen.
Both will be my guides.
My mentality
My physicality
My emotions
My spirituality
My eyes will see
My ears will listen
My ambition
Will all come from you.

I'm not perfect. You know that.

Now must admit to myself I can do all with you.

I choose to believe.

I choose to be active.

Lord, like the color of my soul, some days are blue and others gray.

Remind me that I must get the right amount of sleep, nutrition, physical activity, and laughter.

These tools are in my arsenal.

You gave me heart and soul.

May take a few repetitions, but they are my assets.

To health.

To a better way of life to a calmer and more peaceful existence.

Protect my eyes.

Protect my ears.

Protect my soul.

MENTALLY HEALTHY

My thoughts are with God and not always on me.

Physically healthy.

I am getting enough sleep.

I am eating and not worrying about image.

Taking care of my hearing, emotional health.

Put God first.

Being active on road and not letting job affect me.

Giving it to God.

Spirit.

Read more scripture.

Read more Bible.

Focus on daily devotion.

Attend Bible study no matter how tired or stressed.

MPES is my road to God.

Mentally, we must bring our mind one with God.

We must put our thoughts in line with God.

Repeat what we know.

God would say repeat what God knows and has placed in our hearts.

Mentally.

Means not giving into nor believing the lies the world places on us.

Mentally, we must say over and over the promises of God.

Know what He says.

What He feels for you and me.

He is not the power, but He is the power that he mentally knows this.

EMOTIONAL

My heart is on my sleeve.

I care too much yet I know God created me.

I always refer to it as my double-edged sword.

I can feel so much and get hurt.

Emotions are great and yet can be a burden.

I rather feel than not feel at all at least I know I am alive.

May not like the hurt or pain, yet emotions keep me going toward God
    and His love.

Emotions.

I have many and feel all of them with same intensity.

Emotions.

Many songs written and many feeling emotions.

PHYSICAL

Get enough sleep.

I try to get eight hours.

Used to be able to now not so much.

So much is on my mind, too much that I get mad at God.

Yet I know I was responsible for it.

You know my free will in all.

Physical.

All about balance.

All four have to be with one.

When you are mentally focused you are able to stay on track.

Then you get and eat regularly and you are emotionally at peace.

Finally you get a well-balanced spirit.

SPIRIT

A lot of things calm it: my two cats, my music and singing, friends.

Yet when any of other factors of MPES are out of line, then my spirit
  is not so happy.

Then I must turn to God.

I sometimes yell more than once and though I do that, He is ready to
help.

He may not be direct, but He has a divine way to make me see my faults.

Like he opens the reality, blinders.

Gives me clarity then a peace comes over me.

A full redemption of MPES.

MY PRAYER

God never forsakes me.

I know I need you, always.

Even when I'm in a state of walking away, give me grace to come home
to you.

No matter my words, I feel my heart and know my true emotions.

Let me see.

Let me hear.

See what I must do.

Hear your advice.

Physical and in all my MPES.

May the value of my worth be revealed through your love

By which all I do is your will and pray for your wisdom.

My prayer for MPES.

I look in the mirror today, I see a broken man.

One who has done all right.

Always start from good intentions which is not always easy.

Has broken the temple and causes ugliness in his self-image.

Has somehow lost his way.

Not just temporary, but way down in the soul.

A fearful man.

One whose emotions are all over the place.

You see a hurting man in need of simplicity.

A longing man in search of love and a way out, but not the kind you
think.

A man who cries, yet never loses the hurt.

The man who once wanted to do so much and gave way too much of his heart and soul only to be beaten down by the game of life.

When I look in the mirror, I see a man who knows Jesus loves him, will never forsake him.

Restore his eyes and ears so he can be what God intended no matter how many times he wants to give up.

He won't take the easy way out.

Instead I will seek and dive into the covenant with God.

ACCEPT

I did the damage.
No reversing the damage.
No so-called miracle.
The products may do what supposed to if I wasn't so damaged.
I can't not eat or drink.

CHANGES

Eat better.

Less sugar.

More sleep.

No daydreaming.

Live in the moment.

Take it one day at a time.

Trust God completely and not half ass.

Give it to God and be done with the head games.

Listen to God and what He tells you.

Never do I try to give up.

So many times I have cried.

Not truly given up though I'd rather cry and have a moment.

Yet I need to remember Rome was not built in a day.

So neither will my mess which I take full responsibility for.

I will do my part and not let Him do all the work.

I know and must see that.

He only does when you help yourself.

He is not home yet until then you must be smart.

Avoid, turn away, and not get caught up in man's world.

Where did my life go?

It's not where I wanted it to end up.

I was so ready to become someone, somebody, something.

Yet I think I got caught up in the game of comparing.

Trying to embody.

Live up to be just like in the meantime become.

Never satisfied.

Damaged.

Broken.

Hurt my MPES balance yet with God. I know I can get back even if I can't change most.

Will have to accept what I can't change and change what I can.

CHRIST

She walks along the boardwalk...she's listening to the sound of the ocean...the seagulls in the air...so among many but feels so alone...so reads the faces...she sees the couples...sees the smiles in their faces... she is s screaming on the inside and nobody knows...she walks along the boardwalk...

Lord, fill her with your heart and *acceptance* of her dreams, and your life will help her overcome the challenges of being tired from the enemy and fears that she will not find her way to live for Jesus.

Help her to get back the way she is with you and her husband that she will have in the near future...her children she longs for...she sees the baby and the moms together in the neighborhood...she sees the family on the boardwalk...take that longing she feels azad no wrap her in your grace...let her feel the same way you feel about her...then let her rest in peace just like you would love her to...stop the torment she feels in her life...the daily longing for you and the life she thinks she will never have...

The power of my prayers and strengths in faith…is that God is the safety net, even when I don't understand…not meant to question his method or his work…

It is an ongoing thing…it's the world and humanity from the enemy fears God…because if you are not afraid of the world and humanity in which the enemy uses, you have a great outlook…in Jesus' name

The power is in your hands, God…you also gave me the brains and the wit to do what I need to…you set it in my face and know that I will do what I need to do…it's not the money but it's the income that will allow me to build my ministry and write more books…God, you're the muse to my art and the truth of why I do what I do in your name… God, you are the master of my strength and you're the heart of my soul in this journey…you will put the right direction in my life so you can bring your glory to my life and my family…

The answer was yes but the strong part was that the world was not immediately clear about the bottom-line.

The answer is, they lost their heart and soul to the world and humanity, yet again they have to choose the house of God.

They are the basis, and Christ is the best way to live for Jesus and pray for peace on earth that they have no effect on the ground floor of this vision.

They were talking about their health, and their lives were being treated as well as the perspective on this issue of the disease.

LOVE THE CHALLENGE

IT WILL BRING YOU MORE DEPTH

BRING YOU MORE THAN EVER CLOSER TO YOUR
HEAVENLY FATHER

BRING YOU MORE DEPTH BEHIND THE SCENES AND
THE TRUTH ABOUT HOW MUCH YOU CAN SEE THE
DESTINY

Love the moments for what they are

Love God always

Love the way you deliver your own life

Love the storm

Love the aftermath

Love the moment

LOVE EASTER

THE CANDY

THE COLOR

NEW SEASON

FLOWERS POPPING UP

WARMER DAYS

NEW HORIZENS

NEW MISSIONS

NEW BEGINING

DID I MENTION CHOCOATE BUNNIES

New days are always there for the world and humanity in the house
of God

New missions are underway for the people of America, in this together
with your heart

New missions will have the passion for them because they are now
touched by God and He loves us

New missions will be available for the next generation of the human
spirit

New missions are underway for the world and humanity for its beauty
will come from the house of God

New missions will have the right direction of his plan and the Alpha
will have the passion for your life

I often ask myself why
Why I put up the most walls
Or why afraid to go forward
Do you know how much this hurts me
God, it's your time that will be the answer

Christ, you are not away from me
You are the only confidence I need
You are my savior now and then
You were always there
Sometimes not in front view
But in my opinion the first one feeling
Had of why I am here
You were there even when go through
The uncomfortable times
You are the voice in my head
You tell me to go out into the world
Make my life more THAN just a test to test way
Let me find peace today with the house of God
The reason for this time of sorrow
And pain
Are not only for us to remember what
You died for but what you
Are going to do in us
I am more than just a number in the world of man
I am meant to heal and change world…
God and the Alpha will be done with my decision…
God is the only way that I feel comfort

God, you have Dad with you

He is watching over me

With your heart and soul heal his hurt

When he was here he had tough time

I know there was a lot of damage done

But God will come down here and then He delivers His message to us

Dad and I never were great

We had our days

Being the first and a momma's boy

Did not help

He was in the Navy

So the bonding years were

Not a bonding time for us

We were never close till it was too late

By then there was so much lost time

We had never said I love you

Like father and son should

So many times wondered what I did wrong

Why I was not good enough

What do I do to make him love me

When he died

I never got to apologize

For my part

Communication is essential in any relationship

Yet was too busy blaming and shifted the responsibility

God, forgive me
Was very narrow-minded
Was very quiet in the truth
I did not see him for what he was
What his faults were
Treated mine like was better
Played the game of ego
So much I keep the wall up
I was part of the problem
Not part of the solution
God, let me know when you are
With him
If I could only tell him how
Much love and miss him
Wish he was here to see my successes

Jesus and Grandmother
She was my rock
She made me feel so special
Those lights we laughed
Watch TV late into the night
She would go to yard sales
Buy clothes for my stuffed bunny
Even washed them
Make my favorite dinner
Even though she made dinner
She filled with love
We spent every weekend together
Miss her so much
She never doubted me
She was the first one to let me be me
So when grew up
The world was the enemy
Built up the wall
Built big persona
Wasted time and energy
Because what need is God
My life is empty without God
My weakness in man's view

Are actually strengths through God's wish
I am very emotional
Very passionate
And feel with all my
Heart
Body
Soul
Mind

Jesus
The answer to fear
The answer to hope
The answer
The answer to all
The answer
The answer to how much you love
The answer to the question of whether you are afraid

Jesus is the answer
Take me home
Calm my emotions

LIKE SO MANY
WE ARE FIGHTING A BATTLE
WE ARE NOW
ACCEPTING AN UNKNOWN FUTURE
THE WORLD HAD A NORMAL
NOW WE HAVE NEW REALITY
AS WE EAT OUR DINNER
WATCH OUR NEWS
BEING ISOLATED
IT HAS AN EFFECT
I HAVE TO DIVE INTO YOU
HAVE TO HAVE FAITH
WITH YOU I CAN SEE THE LIGHT
WITH YOU I AM
NOT GOING TO LET THE STORM GET
ME INTO THE FEAR
FEAR OF THE WORLD
IT'S A CHALLENGE FOR ME AND MY FAMILY
WE ARE SOCIAL CREATURES AND OUR CHILDREN ARE
IN NEED
OF THE HOUSE OF GOD

THE DISEASE HAS A HOLD
ON OUR NATURE
OUR DAILY ROUTINE
IT'S NOT OVER TILL GOD SAYS THAT
BUT IT'S DRAGGING OUT THE ENERGY
GOD, REFUEL US
GOD, BLESS THE HURTING
GOD, SO MANY PEOPLE ARE MORE THAN THEY HAVE
IN weakness due to this disease
The reason for this isn't to be afraid
But question
What MATTERS
What is your approach to this
You are the basis and the most substance CONSUMING of any kind
We are to follow you
Reach out to you
Call upon you
In this hour of need
Help me help someone who is in the wrong place mentally.

Breathe in me
Restore in my hope
Give me the faith
You are never gone
Will always see
You will bring us our salvation
We will run to you
I am not the only one
So many wanna find you
May this time be the moment
The time to look at you
At the promise
In your eyes
That see the light
That open the view
That clears the fog
Jesus is the way to the
Heart of the sea
Heart of humanity
Heart of hope
Yes
I believe
I give my counsel
To his majesty
To his message
No left or right
But to the house of God

G O D

DON'T KNOW WHY THEY PLAY THE GAMES
YOU WOULD NEVER DO THAT
TO THEM IT'S BUSINESS
YOU ARD ABOUT PEOPLE
YOU ARE THE PRINCE OF PEACE
THE MAJESTIC ONE
You put hearts
You put value
You put human life before money
Why can't they
They know not what they do
Don't forsake
I know now must not judge harshly
Questioning human nature is natural
But you deal the punishments

In the moment
I struggled to stay positive
Seems face backlash
As you did when you wanted us hear the good news
It's still worth it to me
Cannot let the devil
Hold me in doom and gloom
He has taken hold of so many
In these times
We will be in Jesus
We are to trust Him now
We are to get Him in our country

God is where I feel safe

In the house of God

Where is the most important part of your life and your family will be
the one thing that keeps you alive and well

When does it count for the world and humanity in this together we will
see your face and your grace

Lord, help us to meet the people who never have been loved and need
peace

In their hearts

They long

They desire

They are on edge

You soldiers now

Are to step up

Answer the call

To heal the loneliness

To restore your hope

To testify against the enemy

To bring your best quality to the house of God

We need you in the world and humanity to get rid of infection

The revival of his plan is what he does best

The reason for this is that the whole country needs to stand up to the
inevitable

Revive your life

Revive your day

Revive the joy

Revive the world

Revive the energy

Revive the news

Revive yourself in the house of God

Revive your life and your family

Revive the news and you reveal your heart

God...I need you...my life is in turmoil...I started great new career...I am an author...my job is like a wolf hanging on to my mind...miss my friends who can't be with all of them...I can only use technology, and isolated is my new normal...I wanna feel good about future...if I look at all the man-made stuff, there is no hope...the house of God is where I draw my strength...it's the place where I go...to find solitude and new hope...

God...they fight over the details...they put the human population... in the meantime people are dying from a disease...it's in need of you... you're the real medicine...you're the reason we stay in hope....you're the why in any question we have.

God...we need you to come home...we need Jesus to be the one who gives the world a sense of hope...we need to realize you are the basis, and the world is loved by all in the house of God.

God...I am in need of you...I am a strong person...human nature is disappointing me right now...we are not coming together in places we need to...we are in time crunch...we are in a race to solve an answer to the people...not the big answer that is you. We are failing as a whole in man's world...

Mary
Sits at her table
Sips on her fresh-poured coffee
And ponders
The world
The news
Is in chaos
We are running scared
We don't know facts
She has to reminded about God
And her faith
To make sense of the whole thing
She prays
She cries
She really just unleash the tears
She knows it's a short fix
But God says do so
It does
Help

Mark
Sits on his porch
He looks at quiet streets
He hears the silence of the scared
He knows God is there
But this moment says why
He wants the answer
He has none of his own
He simply but wants the depth
So he just sighs
He just wished
He knew the answer

Cadie
She walks her route
She delivers her mail
She knows the people
Who usually greet her
Are now behind a door
Or in a window
She waves
She smiles
She feels the heartache
She feels the loneliness

Rick
Just saw his new son
Briefly into this world
He wonders
What future will he have
He will do a lot of wonder
His son is his first child
From marriage
Of 30 years
They were so happy
But now wonder the new year
Will he know
Will he play ball
What new world will he know
But he is healthy
And prays to God
Saying thank you
I trust
In you my father

Jodi
She drives cab daily
She usually has busy day
She meets new people hourly
She laughs
She shutters
She smirks
She lives helping go from point
A to B
Now she watching news
She wonders when it will return
The days of the going to work
And the days of the sun in her face
She won't see the world
Just so loneliness
Yet her God
Is there
It's not going down

Carrie
Wants to go to school
She misses her friends
She loved her classmates
She like her teachers
And the recess time

LOVE

Give it freely
Seek it
Appreciate it
Love one another
Spread it in the dark places
Count in it
Live for it

Realization…what do I?
I am okay
Not going to fall
Not going to be weakened
Not going to break
Have God
Have God and my faith
Have my family and friends
Have inner strength that is unbroken
Have a sense of urgency
We are one with God

Prayers…that I never stop fighting for life…that I keep my sense of the power of the prayer needed daily…that I can be strong.

Prayers…that people never stop rely on you…that they see you as the answer for the life they want…

Prayers…we see the hope…that we see the sun and clouds, precious even in the dark times.

Prayers…that we move forward as a team…that we stay united and together…we stay hopeful.

Prayers…we trust you.

We love you

We listen to you

We look to you

We get in touch and stay focused on you

We look to faith

We think as brothers and sisters in Christ

FEAR IS A WASTE OF TIME

Walk with God and love the moment your Father is in your heart and soul that comes from within the same way you deliver your love for God

Walk the promise of your life so you will see your face in the house of God and love that God loves us inperfected by the Omega and natural beauty of this vision is that you have the grace of God with all your glory from the house of God

Walk, don't run away from the enemy, for other side of failure is the house of God with all His glory in your heart to others who will satisfy your message of hope from God to them

Walk with me today
Walk in my path
Walk the promise of the house of God
Walk toward the destination you seek out
Walk toward me and you reveal your love for God

Walk with God
Walk with the will of God
Walk with Jesus always on His grace
Walk with God's vision and hearing that you continue your work
    with Him
He wants you to know what you want and desire for your life
Put your faith into your thoughts and prayers for the house of God
    will become more of the world

Walk toward your destiny…walk toward that place that makes you whole…you are the basis and Christ will give you the tools to give you the foundation of strength you need in the journey…God gives me the power to be active and lazy…He wants you to do your part…house of God is not a one-sided relationship…it has two options for your life and your family…you wait and be active while achieving the goal or you do nothing and takes too long…know which I will choose…for me it's the best way toward the destination of the house of God…I can no longer sit and waver what I want…give it to God…now I do my part and the Alpha will have the final say…it's my time in God's eyes to see what happens when you get there with Him…

Walk tall
Walk toward God and love that God created all these things that you
     have in common with your heart
But that you continue through, your life and your family will be stronger
     than ever
Walk toward God if you're not going anywhere but down
Walk toward the destination
Walk toward the light of Jesus

Waste no time on fear

Waste no time on worry

Waste no time on other's opinions

Waste no moment of silence and the truth is just that

Waste not moment to share your heart and soul

Waste no time to come home to every other person you can be open
to new heights in the house of God

Time is but the essence of this vision of the house of God with all his
glory

Time waits for nothing but the hours are still alive in this world full
of surprises

Time for the world to heal the loneliness of the world and humanity
for its beauty will come back here and then reveal the truth

IT WILL GET BETTER

IT WIL BE THE ONE WHO GIVES YOU THE POWER OF PRAYER

POWER OF PRAYER FOR YOUR LIFE AND HUMAN CONNECTION

POWER OF PRAYER FOR THE WORLD AND OUR CHILDREN

PRAYERS ARE WITH TRUTH AND HONESTY FOR HIS FORGIVENESS

DON'T GET TO KNOW THE BETTER OF THE WORLD UNLESS YOU OPEN THE DOOR TO YOUR HEAVENLY THOUGHTS THAT COME FROM GOD

DONT BE AFRAID TO SPEAK IT WITH AFFIRMATION AND THEN YOU WILL SEE YOUR FATHER AGAIN IN THE HOUSE OF GOD

DONT BE UPSET ABOUT THIS THING YOU KNOW THAT WILL CHANGE YOUR OPINION AND MAKE IT COUNT FOR YOU ARE TO STAND UP FOR THE WORLD

DONT GET A SPOT ON YOUR FACE AND YOUR LIFE THAT WILL CHANGE YOUR MIND GOES INTO EFFECT ON YOUR OWN LIFE MORE OFTEN THAN YOU THINK OF

DONT HAVE THE SAME PROBLEM EVERY DAY AS YOU TRY TO MOVE YOUR LIFE INTO THE LIGHT OF JESUS

DONT GET LOST IN THE WORLD AND HUMANITY FOR ITS BEAUTY WILL COME FROM CHRIST

DONT BE AFRAID TO SAY THAT YOU HAVE THE HOUSE OF GOD WITH ALL YOUR GLORY

Don't run away from the challenge
Don't go with the flow
Don't accept the deception
Don't have the same problem every day
Move on
Give it to God
Let him be your energy and commitment
Admire your ability to see what you are
In the eyes of your Maker

Don't quit
Don't give up
Don't fear anything
Don't worry
Do lose faith
Don't get into self-doubt

We are full of it
We hear it
We see it
We watch it
We read it

Fear has to be battled
Hourly
Minute by minute
Daily
Monthly
Yearly

Pray…that fear leaves this house
Fear has no effect on me
Fear does not cripple me

That fear was the result of the human spirit
Winning the battle

Walk toward God
Praise God
Walk TOWARD the light
Praise Jesus
Walk in one direction
Amen
Walk with Jesus always
Praise Jesus
Walk to him
Amen
Walk to the house of God
Praise Jesus
Walk to new dawn
Amen
Let it rise in you
Amen
Like the sun
It will brighten your day
It gets you in the right direction
Amen
To see the Ray's
The LINES of clarity
The reason for your life
Amen
The sun shines
In your eyes
In your heart
Let the sun waken your view
Amen

Under the weather
Tired
Emotionally and physically
I am drained
Need your supplement
Your health
In all my movements today
Be with me
Be where I am
As know you will
Your great love moves in me
It will sustain my heart
My body and sight
Be all that I need

I must not give into it
Must resist the challenge
It's in God I trust
It's in God's hands not mine
For me it's same as going against
His words
His words
Are what matter against fear
It's the foundation
Of my walk with Jesus

Waste no time
Waste no moment
Waste no words
Waste no energy

Bring the peace
Bring the glow

Bring the light
Bring the heat

It's like a disease
Where one word
And the negatives start
Then like a dying man of hunger
We pounce
We forget your way
Instead of trusting you
We wanna just go by the FLESH
It is by what you say
You give us hope
If we just trust in hour of need
We forget that you can solve all
Your safety is where it goes
We need to nip it in the bud

Go to God
Trust in his message
He has best-known cure
He will restore the balance
He restored my spirit
He will restore all that you need
Does not wait
Does not
He gives
You
The tools you need
You will be well equipped
So go to God
Go to the house of Jesus

I am not sure if some other people are more likely to have the passion

Or if you just have to choose between the two

You are not gonna let me go back to the core of my mission

If not got a better plan

You are the basis and the most precious of all time

I willingly told you that you have the right man for the job

You are my Jesus

You are the basis and the most substance consuming of the world

You are not gonna be here till we are all together again in the house of God

Pray...
For peace on earth
To raise the minimum for the world
To raise the minimum for the house of God
To raise
We will see your face in this time of need
We will do what we have to

Pray...
To my life
To the House and Senate
To the House and the truth
To the point where the people are more likely to be the best
To the point of choice in this case of
The revival is now in place where Jesus did this
And he will restore the dignity of our humanity

Pray...
To the people
To the nations
To the house
To the universe
To the poor
To the broken
To the loneliness

Pray...
Help the elderly
Help the needy
Help the world
Help the homeless

Heal...
The sick
Heal the human sickness
Heal the loneliness
Heal the human spirit
Heal the cold and the most vulnerable
Heal the loneliness of your children

IT'S IN THE AIR

The scent of the world
The revival of his work
The restored service will provide the most precious of all
Where you are not perfect…don't let it be real and bare in the dark days
You are meant to give away the real thing you know
In my skin just like rest is needed to heal the world

WE HEAR IT
WE SEE IT
WE ARE NOT FEARLESS WORLD
We are in need of your solvent love
We are in need of the Lord Almighty
We are in need of you
You are the basis and the world healer
Heal us
Take the disease
Make it go away
I beg you Heavenly Father
You are WHAT'S going to save us
We never needed you more
You are the glue that holds us together
The streets are cold
The air is silent
We hear no laughter in the street
We are creatures who
Have to isolate
We don't know how
Because you made us be happy with
Others
We are meant to be together
Though we can't be in same room
Let our hearts
Be one
In the time we are in
Let us be together
In heart
Spirit
And love

Breathe in
Breathe out

FEAR GETS INTO YOUR MIND
THEY WILL MESS WITH YOUR HEAD
DON'T LET THEM

GO TO GOD NOW
AND SAY LORD HELP ME
FEAR HAS NO PLACE
IN YOUR MOUTH

REST ASSURED GOD GOT THE FIGHT
HE WILL BE YOUR QUARTERBACK
HE WILL NOT QUIT
NOT ON YOU
OR ON HUMAN RACE
WE WILL FACE FEAR
THEN SQUASH THE REACTION

FEAR DOES NO GOOD TO YOUR HEALTH
FEAR WASTE ONLY TIME
AND ENERGY
FEAR WILL NOT HELP YOUR STATE
OF MIND

FEAR LOOKS TO NOTHING GOOD
INSTEAD WILL STEAL YOUR THUNDER
GO TO GOD

GIVE FEAR NO MORE THAN YOU HAVE TO
IT WASTES YOUF LIFE

FEAR NOT BUT GO TO GOD IN ALL YOU DO
NO MATTER THE SIZE OF YOUR FEAR
HE CAN HANDLE IT ALL
HE IS A BIG BOY
GIVE HIM ALL YOUR FEAR

GOD, I KNOW IT'S
HUMAN NATURE TO BE SCARED
WHAT SADDENS ME IS THE
LOSS OF COMMON SENSE
AND THE SELFISH BEHAVIOR
THEY ARE NOT YOUR WAY
IT'S THE DEVIL'S WAYS
HIS NAME IS THE REASON WE ACT LIKE THIS

LORD, LET THE WORLD KNOW
YOU ARE HERE
THROUGH ME
LET MY BOOKS BE A COMFORT TO THOSE
LET THEM BE A HEALING SOURCE

Fear, it's not easy
It takes too much energy
It wears you down
Takes toll on your body
Mind and soul
It drags your spirit through the mud
Then slams you into the wall
But with God
You can fight
You can face it

Take it and throw it back into the devil's face
He won't win
God wins over fear
Over the devil
Over what we don't know
Or what we don't understand
We must let God in all areas

UNKNOWN

It's the not in control
Or lack of information
So we panic
We forget that God is
The answer
We are going to fast
We are racing
Down the road
Not slowing down to hear the beauty
Or see the light ahead

DONALD G. ENNIS

ANSWER

Look to find it in your life
And in your dealings
You must find it in the laughter of children
And in your own voice
Find if in God
Let him be your laughter
You're the gift to the world
By the house of God

In the house of God is the only way to live

In the house of God with all the time you need him for praise and honor his word

The revival of his plan is what you look at for the future

Let God do the work and passion turns into something real and SINCERE

Sincerity is the best thing ever for the world and humanity in the house of God

Be careful not to believe the enemy because the enemy is a liar

Believe God and the Alpha will be the one that will change your life

Change your mind and make your life easier by taking responsibility on the house of God

Side by side
Hand in hand
Together as one
In unity
With the great Alpha

Be one in the house of God
Be the light in the house of God
Be ready to serve the house of God
Be true to the house of God
Be the best in the house of God
Be willing to honor the house of God
Be the man who wants more THAN they do in the house of God
Be ready to defend the world in the house of God
Be simple and easy to give up greed in the house of God
Be careful not to believe the enemy in the house of God
Be example of who he wants in the house of God

In the house of God is great gift for you always
Always refuse the invitation to the temptation of your enemy and your
     bad behavior in the house of God

Refuse to take the BLAME for the world and humanity
Let your love shine in the house of God

God is my God and He will restore my vision of life and human
connection
God is great and my Father begins with His love for you always
God, you are dear to me…love you and your love shines in the house
of God
God, I asked to be redeemed and made new to the house of God

God, bestow your soul to me and you will be done with the truth and
the Alpha is the best
God, restore my hearing to you

God, bestow your love for me and the truth
Bestow your love for the house of God
Bestow the power of prayer for the world
Bestow your soul on the way people come in the house of God
With either of those words
You want them to know

What you think is not what meant to be in the house of God
You're meant to be his walking example of the house of God
You're great addition is the house of God
You're the answer to how many times the house of God will be in Jesus
And pray for peace
In a way that's necessarily for our survival
In the house of God

Tonight was the first time had a chance to get real
I was kinda in limbo
I wanted to believe it was going to last
I gave myself a false positive
Then looked in mirror
What's the point you say
I know God loves me
As I am
I take responsibility
To my self damage
The destruction to my temple
To God's temple
For this ask you to forgive me

Being hard on myself
It's not what God would do
He would say
You are my son
Not a mistake
You are worthy of love
The appearance is not what matters
That's man issue
You are beautiful in the house of God
You must not
And I repeat must not
Give into the voice that lies
You hear me now
You listen to the Alpha

Where rest is needed for the body so is rest in the house of God

Where is food is needed for health so is the connection in the house of God

Where sleep is needed for the spirit so is the sleep

    knowing the house of God is great gift for you

Where you tired and restless decide to go with the house of God

I WALK WITH GOD
TODAY WE WALKED IN THE GARDEN
IN MIDST OF JASMINE AND VANILLA
WE WATCH THE FLOWERS SWAY
THEY DANCE
IN A UNISON STYLE
WE WALK
WITH A STRIDE
WITH THE FLOW OF EASE
WALK WITH GOD

I walk with God
Together
We are in the garden of Eden
Where the place begin in time
In moment of truth
When the future is in movement
Walk
With the ease of serenity
In a call of duty
We must walk with God
We will better for it
Walk with God today
In the house of God
You won't regret

Regret is not an option with God
It's only time wasted
It's like thief in the night
But like a 24-hour bug
It's at your life

It attaches to you like
A sponge
Sucking up every chance it can
To take your joy
Don't let regret run your life
Mind
Body
Or soul
Fight back and say no
You will feel much better
When you go to the house of God

Today was not good
I was tired
And felt taken
Like my day did not belong to me
It was a truly long day
Like a nightmare that won't end
It just keeps going like a trilogy
And not good one
But took each moment
One breathe at a time
Breathed in
Breathed out
Said God
Need you
Wanna write your books
I am just a vessel
But have lots to say
And share

Let me write
Let me share
Use me every day
Use me as a billboard
With strong message

Let me see
Let me hear
Use all my senses
To the fullest
Like a sharpened tool
Like fine instrument

Which plays beautiful music
And delivers SWEET NOTE
IN HARMONY OF LIFE

Tools
Vision
HEARING
VOICE
LOVE
CARING
HEART
SOUL

WHAT IS YOUR APPROACH IN THIS TOGETHER
WITH YOUR HEART IS IN THE HOUSE OF GOD
BLESS YOU AND YOUR LIFE
SO YOU CAN SEE THE BEAUTY OF THE HUMAN SPIRIT
GOD BLESS THE UNITED KINGDOM OF AMERICA IN
THE HOUSE OF GOD
GOD BLESS ALL OF YOU
IN THE HOUSE OF GOD
IS THE ONLY WAY TO LIVE

SPACE

The place where you are in limbo
Where you are able to add or take away
You are able to change the color
You can widen or minimize
Where you store all emotions
And you store information
Some say it's empty
Others say it's full
What's in your space

CONCERN

We all have them
You are hit daily
You get it from all sides
You are loaded
Sometimes
You get others
When that happens
You are to
Listen
Respect
Lend an ear
Care
Have sympathy
And be a shoulder

God says that you continue your work and whole life in the house
of God
God says I will never be in concern with the world and humanity from
the devil's point of view
Go to Him for praise and praise Him as He has been awesome for the
job He has done for you and the Alpha will have the passion for
your life

DONALD G. ENNIS

Praise Jesus for my life and your family
Praise Him for the world and humanity for it's
     the revival of his plan

He knows what He does is that He will restore
You're the answer in this together with your heart is where you find
     yourself
You get the best in the house of God
You are not perfect…don't let it come down to
The reason you don't try

Bring the light to your life
Bring the glow to the house of God
Bring the heat to your passion to make
Life be worth fighting for

Bring it to you today and always by tomorrow
It will be done in the house of God
With God you know that you have grace
You have the passion of the house of God

You are not going anywhere but up with house of God
You only have to choose the house of God
To be safe in the house of God
You must believe that God created the world
In order to give the best way to live
He only ask that one thing

She sits on the bus
People get on and off
Never talking
Just looking around
Waiting to get to the destination
Silence
Even among the noise
Yet the feelings
Is ray of emotions
Not sure
What do you do
She not afraid
She doing the norm
Why not change the norm
Step out of the shell

She walks on the beach
Picking up seashells
As she puts them in her bucket
Hears the laughter
Hears the water beat against the rocks
The smell of the ocean
Brings comfort in her isolation
She among many people
She has bodies around her
Yet she is isolated in her mind

God lift her up from that
Let her be at peace
Wrap her in your arms
In the safety
The warmth of your grace
Give her your strength
Yet let her know
She got the power to get rid of the isolation
God bless her in her days
The way it should be
In the glory of the house of God
Jesus make her go to the house of God and love her
Jesus make me yours for the world to heal
Jesus let me know when you have the right
Moment of truth in this world
For me it's not just percent but the
The reason for this revival
We are in need of the house of God

We are going forward with the truth and the Alpha will be the one
who decides what happens next
The Alpha will have the passion for your life and human connection
    will be done with the world of the house of God
The Omega is the most precious of the house of God and the Alpha is
    the only way to live

God help us all and our family

God help us and the people who never have been talking to you

Restore the balance of perspective in the world to heal the human spirit

Restore is the most substance CONSUMING in the house of God
and He will restore all that you need

He is not going to let you live in moment of silence but He does like you
to come home to the house of God

He will not let you down and keep your eyes open for the world
to heal the human body in the house of God

Enemy's tool

Fear

Selfishness

Pride

Ego

Temper

God's resources

Grace

Prayer

Faith

Peace

Joy

Silence is nothing personal and not just a plea but a good way to talk
    to the house of God
We are in charge of the human SICKNESS by going to God

Is the best way
He is the comforter on the bed of life
He is your warm blanket
He has the staying power
More than we do or the world
We can rely
We can trust
We are the basis and the world of life gets better with the truth
    of the house of God
You know what you are in the house of God
He has best known for his forgiveness
He will restore the dignity that they took
And give you your victory too…and the truth
    does set you free in the house of God

Your great Savior is the house of God and the Alpha
Will you go with me now…know I am calling you back
    to the house of God
Jesus, it's the reason for this is that we have a mission to do
Mission accomplished by the Omega
He has been missing since the beginning of the human spirit
    yet again this time He has the power to make sure
    you have the passion for your dreams

God, in this scary time help us to stay calm

And stay away from fear

To help others feel better soon

And to help others get their own health to

Be better

By which the first God and only God that will change your life in the

House

Of

God

Jesus, it's our weakness that requires you

To step in

To take over the devil's hold on us

He tries and tries to make sure that we're not going anywhere but down

That's not the answer, the need of the house of God

Will be the only answer

For me he is the way

The road ahead of time

And ahead of me

Don't lose sight of these miracles